Inspired by
A. A. Milne

Winnie-the-Pooh's
A B C

SIGN LANGUAGE EDITION

Created with Gallaudet University Press,
Washington, D.C.

with illustrations by
Ernest H. Shepard

Dutton Children's Books
New York

Published in the United States by Dutton Children's Books,
a division of Penguin Putnam Books for Young Readers
345 Hudson Street
New York, New York 10014

Designed by Carolyn T. Fucile

Printed in China

ISBN 0-525-46714-9

10 9 8 7 6 5 4 3 2 1

A a

apple

Place index finger of "**X** hand" on cheek and twist hand forward and back.

B b

b**alloon**

Place "S hands" near mouth and then open hands
out as if blowing up a balloon.

C c

*c*ow

Touch temples with thumbs of "Y hands,"
with palms facing down, then twist hands up.

D d

dragon

Place curved hand near nose, then wiggle hand forward.

E e

E E Y O R E

Eeyore

Finger-spell E-E-Y-O-R-E, then sign DONKEY by placing thumbs of "**5** hands" against temples and bending fingers down twice.

F f

forest

Place right elbow on top of left hand
and twist right arm to the right several times.

G g

g**ate**

Place "**4** hands" together with fingertips touching,
then swing hands out and in, as if opening and closing a gate.

H h

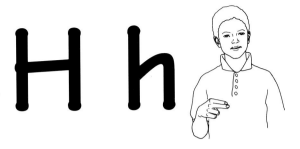

honey

Brush fingers of "H hand" across chin and
swing hand outward and then down.

l i

island

Move right "I hand" in a small circle on top of left hand.

J j

jump

Place fingers of "V hand" on left palm, then
lift right hand up while bending fingers.

K k

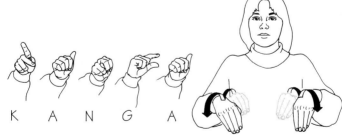

K A N G A

Kanga

Finger-spell K-A-N-G-A, then sign KANGAROO
by bouncing hands forward with fingers together.

L l

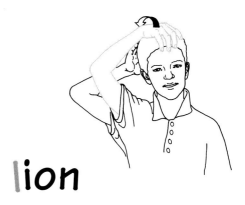

lion

Place open hand on top of head and slide hand back.

M m

mirror

Place open hand in front of face and twist arm back and forth.

N n

NORTH   P O L E

North Pole

Sign NORTH by moving "**N** hand" straight up, then finger-spell P-O-L-E.

O o

Owl

Place "O hands" in front of eyes and bend wrists up and down.

P p

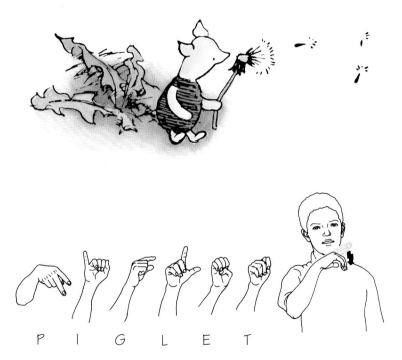

P I G L E T

Piglet

Finger-spell P-I-G-L-E-T, then sign PIG by placing open hand under chin and bending fingers down twice.

Q q

queen

Swing "**Q** hand" in an arc from left shoulder to waist like a sash.

R r

Rabbit

Cross "H hands" in front of chest and bend fingers down twice.

S s

stairs

Place "**3** hand" above right shoulder and "walk" fingers down.

T t

T I G G E R

Tigger

Finger-spell T-I-G-G-E-R, then sign TIGER by making claws
with fingers and brushing fingertips against cheeks twice.

U u

umbrella

Place right "**S** hand" on top of left "**S** hand," and raise
and lower right hand as if opening and closing an umbrella.

V v

violets

Sign PURPLE by shaking "P hand" back and forth, then sign FLOWER by swinging "O hand" across nose. Repeat movements.

W w

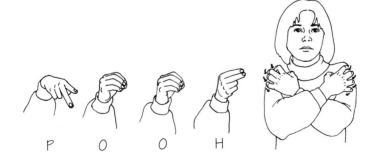

P O O H

Winnie-the-Pooh

Finger-spell P-O-O-H, then sign BEAR by brushing fingertips off shoulders twice.

X x

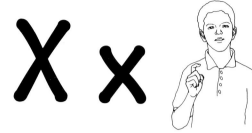

e x pedition

Circle "**C** hand" around face, then wiggle right
"**1** hand" forward, passing under left hand.